STEM CAREERS
BIOLOGIST

by R.J. Bailey

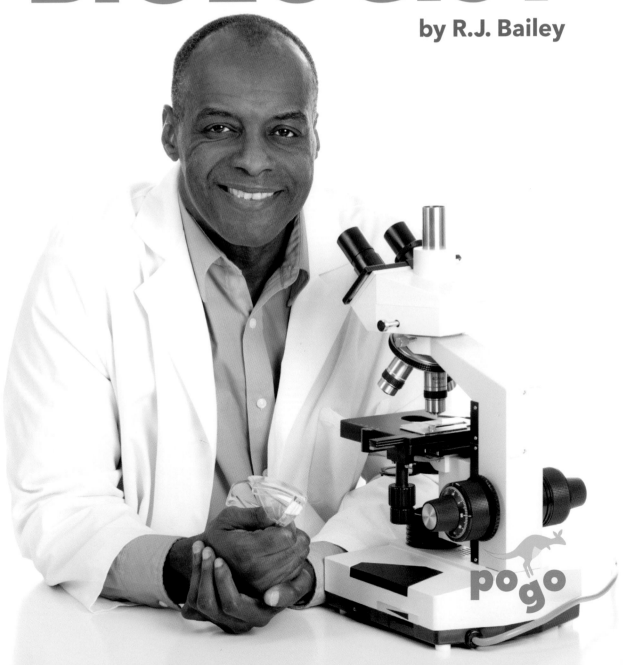

pogo

Ideas for Parents and Teachers

Pogo Books let children practice reading informational text while introducing them to nonfiction features such as headings, labels, sidebars, maps, and diagrams, as well as a table of contents, glossary, and index.

Carefully leveled text with a strong photo match offers early fluent readers the support they need to succeed.

Before Reading

- "Walk" through the book and point out the various nonfiction features. Ask the student what purpose each feature serves.
- Look at the glossary together. Read and discuss the words.

Read the Book

- Have the child read the book independently.
- Invite him or her to list questions that arise from reading.

After Reading

- Discuss the child's questions. Talk about how he or she might find answers to those questions.
- Prompt the child to think more. Ask: Do you know anyone who works as a biologist? What projects has he or she been involved in? Do you have any interest in this kind of work?

Pogo Books are published by Jump!
5357 Penn Avenue South
Minneapolis, MN 55419
www.jumplibrary.com

Library of Congress Cataloging-in-Publication Data

Names: Bailey, R.J., author.
Title: Biologist / by R.J. Bailey.
Description: Minneapolis, MN: Jump!, Inc., [2017]
Series: STEM careers | Audience: Ages 7-10.
Includes bibliographical references and index.
Identifiers: LCCN 2017007349 (print)
LCCN 2017009932 (ebook)
ISBN 9781620317136 (hardcover: alk. paper)
ISBN 9781624965906 (ebook)
Subjects: LCSH: Biology–Vocational guidance–Juvenile literature. | Biologists–Juvenile literature.
Classification: LCC QH309.2 .B345 2017 (print)
LCC QH309.2 (ebook) | DDC 570.23–dc23
LC record available at https://lccn.loc.gov/2017007349

Editor: Jenny Fretland VanVoorst
Book Designer: Michelle Sonnek
Photo Researcher: Michelle Sonnek

Photo Credits: Adobe Stock: Kateryna_Kon, 5. Getty: IMAGEMORE Co, Ltd., 5; Sean Justice, 10; Romulic-Stojcic, 11. iStock: cglade, 1; asiseeit, 19. Shutterstock: Nata-Lia, cover; I love photo, 3; Julia Reschke, 3; Seaphotoart, 4; diplomedia, 6-7; wavebreakmedia, 8-9; anyaivanova, 12-13; Budimir Jevtic, 14-15; espies, 18; all_about_people, 20-21; Africa Studio, 23. SuperStock: Blue Jean Images, 16-17.

Printed in the United States of America at Corporate Graphics in North Mankato, Minnesota.

TABLE OF CONTENTS

CHAPTER 1
LIFE LEARNERS

Life is everywhere. It is in the water. It is in the air. It is in the harshest deserts on Earth.

Even your own body is covered with tiny life forms!

Biologists study life. Some study animals. Others study bones. Some study plants. Others study **cells** and **bacteria**. There are even biologists who study crime scenes!

Why do biologists study life? They are curious about our world. They want to understand the similarities all life forms share. They want to solve problems like disease and hunger.

DID YOU KNOW?

At the **genetic** level, living things look very similar. For example, your **genetic code** looks a lot like that of a flower!

CHAPTER 2

WHAT DO THEY DO?

Biologists work in different settings. Some spend time outside. This is called working "in the field."

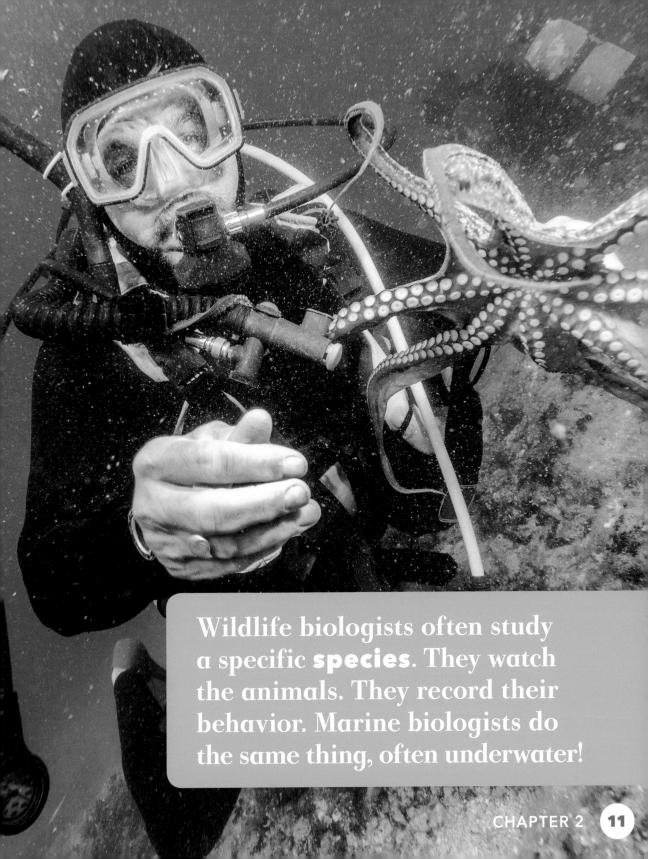

Wildlife biologists often study a specific **species**. They watch the animals. They record their behavior. Marine biologists do the same thing, often underwater!

Other biologists spend most of their time in a lab. They use microscopes to see tiny life forms. They use test tubes. They use **beakers**. They use **forceps** and **probes**. These tools help them handle delicate **specimens**.

Biologists use microscopes. These tools help them see things invisible to the unaided eye.

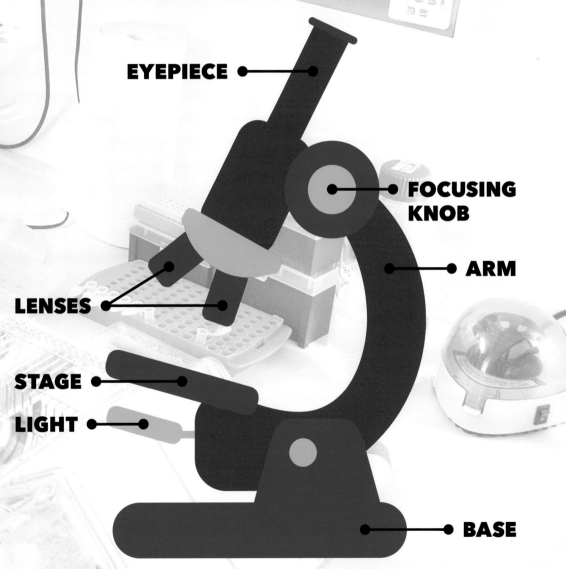

EYEPIECE

FOCUSING KNOB

ARM

LENSES

STAGE

LIGHT

BASE

They also use tools special to their area. Marine biologists use a camera that works in water. A **botanist** uses a magnifying glass. Why? This makes it easy to see plants up close.

DID YOU KNOW?

Plant biologists are called botanists. Those who study the tiniest life forms are microbiologists. Some create medical devices that help people who are sick or hurt. They are bioengineers.

magnifying
glass

Most biologists use computers to study **data**. Then they report their findings. They write articles. They talk with other scientists.

CHAPTER 3

BECOMING A BIOLOGIST

Do you want to be a biologist? Having a curious mind is important.

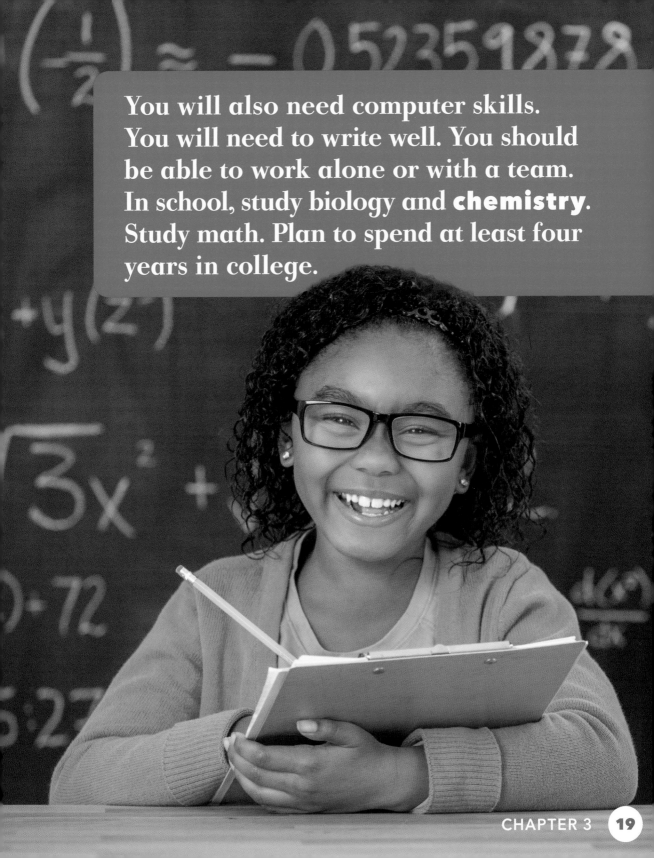

You will also need computer skills. You will need to write well. You should be able to work alone or with a team. In school, study biology and **chemistry**. Study math. Plan to spend at least four years in college.

As a biologist, you can shape the future. How? You could end a disease. You could save a species from **extinction**. You could find new ways to feed the hungry. The things you can do are endless!

DID YOU KNOW?

To work as a biologist, you need STEM skills. What does STEM stand for? Science. Technology. Engineering. Math. STEM careers are in demand. They pay well, too.

ACTIVITIES & TOOLS

TRY THIS!

LIQUID GROWTH

Did you know you can plant seeds in just liquid? In this activity, you will learn which liquids are better for sprouting seeds.

You Will Need:
- 1 cup each of tap water, cool tea, milk, and vinegar
- four glass or plastic cups, the same color and size
- one package of bean seeds
- permanent marker
- tray or shallow pan
- ruler and paper towels

① **Use the permanent marker to label each cup by the liquid it holds.**

② **Put the cups on the tray and pour each liquid into its own cup.**

③ **Open the bean seed package. Divide them evenly into four piles.**

④ **Add one seed pile to each of the four cups.**

⑤ **Place the tray where you can watch the seeds. Make sure it is in an area where there are no drafts from windows or doors.**

⑥ **Each day, write down what you see.**

⑦ **In seven days, measure the length of each sprout in centimeters. If your seeds haven't sprouted, measure them again in two weeks. To make this easier, place a sprout on a paper towel.**

⑧ **What happened? Which liquid(s) do your bean sprouts "like" best? Why do you think that is?**

GLOSSARY

bacteria: Single-celled life forms that live in soil, water, plants, and animals and that sometimes cause disease.

beakers: Deep glasses with a wide mouth and usually a lip for pouring.

botanist: A biologist who studies plants.

cells: Tiny parts that are the building blocks of all life forms.

chemistry: A science that deals with the structure of substances and the changes that they go through.

data: Facts about something.

extinction: The situation that results when a type of plant or animal has died out completely.

forceps: Tools that are used for grasping or holding things.

genetic: Having to do with genes, the parts of cells that control or influence inherited traits such as height or eye color.

genetic code: The arrangement of genes that makes a life form develop in a special way.

grants: Gifts of money to be used for a particular purpose.

probes: Tools that are used to touch and examine something.

proposals: Written plans that are given to a person or group of people to consider.

species: A grouping of things of the same kind and with the same name that are able to reproduce to create fertile offspring.

specimens: Materials being tested or examined.

INDEX

TO LEARN MORE

Learning more is as easy as 1, 2, 3.

1) Go to www.factsurfer.com

2) Enter "biologist" into the search box.

3) Click the "Surf" button to see a list of websites.

With factsurfer, finding more information is just a click away.